SCHOLASTIC

FIRST
picture
DICTIONARY

Cartwheel BOOKS®

an imprint of

SCHOLASTIC

www.scholastic.com

New York · Toronto · London · Auckland · Sydney · Mexico City · New Delhi · Hong Kong

CONTENTS

The body

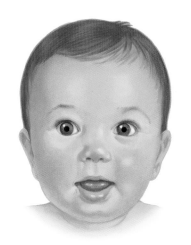

In the house

At school

In the city

At the grocery store

Exploring nature

Index

THE FACE

Question

Which baby is sticking out his tongue and closing his eyes at the same time?

Answer: the baby on the bottom right side of this page

hair

forehead

eye

cheek

mouth

ear

dimple

chin

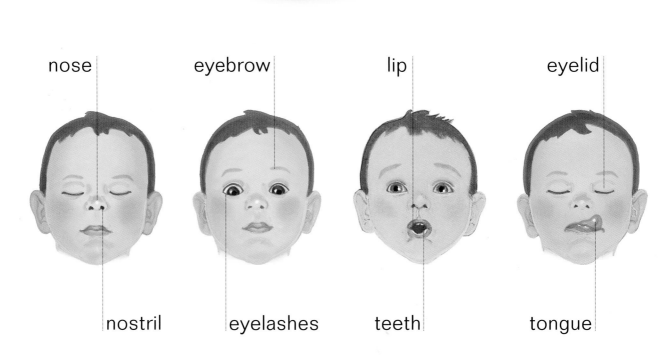

nose

eyebrow

lip

eyelid

nostril

eyelashes

teeth

tongue

THE HAND

pinky

palm

ring finger

thumb

middle finger

index finger

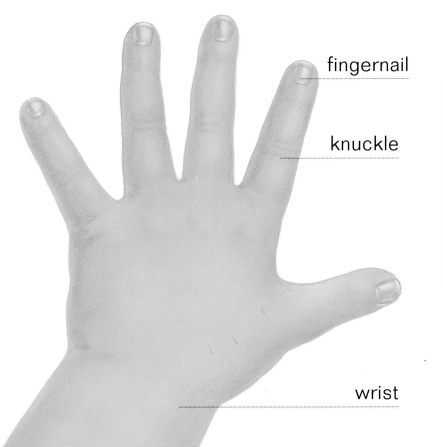

fingernail

knuckle

Did you know?

The fourth finger is called the ring finger because that's where people traditionally wear their wedding rings.

wrist

CLOTHES

pajamas

nightgown

bathrobe

briefs

underwear

boxers

socks

kneesocks

slippers

tights

jeans

pants

overalls

dress

skirt

tank top

T-shirt

polo shirt

button-down shirt

sweatshirt

sweater

cardigan

CLOTHES

jacket

raincoat

umbrella

parka

down jacket

coat

scarf

glove

cap

hat

handbag

belt

suspenders

baseball cap

watch

bracelet

ring

necklace

glasses

shoe

sandal

sneaker

boot

THE BEDROOM

chair

table

curtains

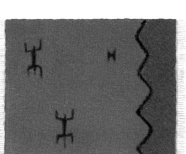

rug

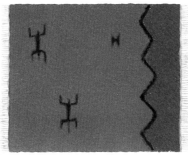

hanger

dresser

armoire

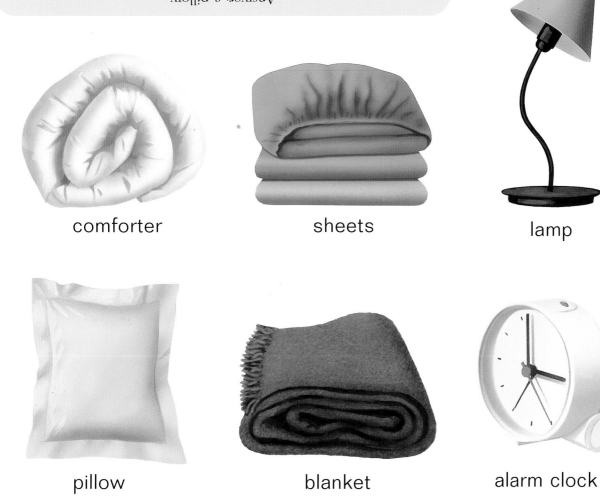

comforter

sheets

lamp

pillow

blanket

alarm clock

bed

radiator

TOYS

book

doll

teddy bear

top

ball

playing cards

block

rocking horse

puzzle

Question

How many black dots are there
on the domino?
How many white dots are there
on the green die?

Answer:
There are 9 black dots on the domino
and 14 white dots on the green die.

robot

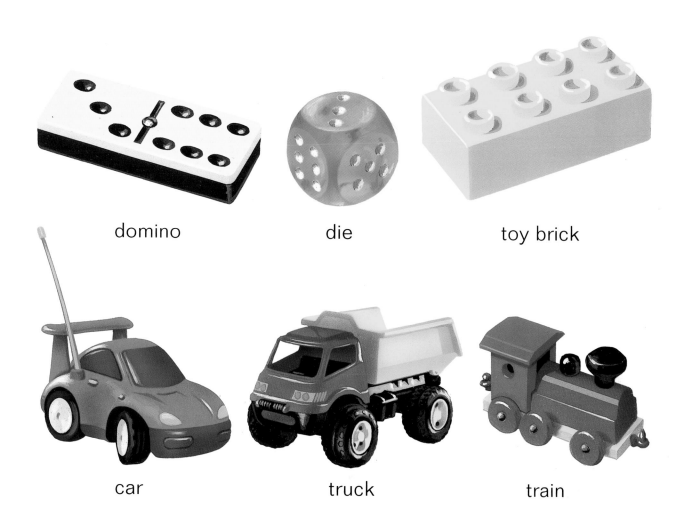

domino

die

toy brick

car

truck

train

THE LIVING ROOM

magazine

comic book

painting

photograph

fireplace

vase

coffee table

sofa

cushion

armchair

remote control   television   computer

VCR

telephone   videotape   DVD player

radio   stereo   CD

THE BATHROOM

sink

bathtub

shower

faucet

potty

toilet

toilet paper

laundry hamper

washer
and dryer

laundry rack

clothespin

soap   conditioner   shampoo   blow-dryer

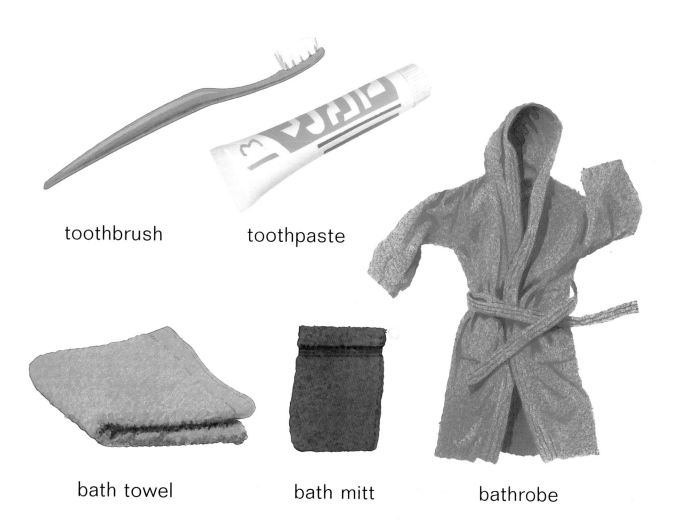

toothbrush   toothpaste

bath towel   bath mitt   bathrobe

THE BATHROOM

razor

shaving brush

shaving lotion

shaving cream

electric razor

perfume

mirror

scale

thermometer

tweezers

nail clippers

scissors

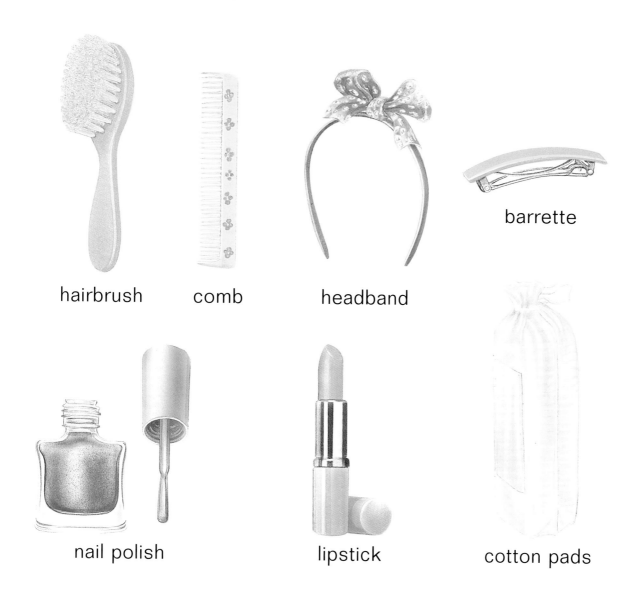

hairbrush   comb   headband

barrette

nail polish   lipstick   cotton pads

bandage   cotton swabs   tissues

THE KITCHEN

kitchen sink

freezer

refrigerator

range

dishwasher

stove

microwave

colander frying pan

lid pot pressure cooker

teapot teakettle coffeemaker

whisk hand blender hand mixer food processor

THE KITCHEN

carving knife

cutting board

bread basket

glass bottle

glass

pitcher

plastic bottle

plate

bowl

cup

eggcup

spoon

fork

knife

ladle

salad servers

spatula

wooden spoon

casserole dish

salad bowl

cake pan

THE KITCHEN

bib

baby bottle

stool

high chair

kitchen scale

toaster

clock

ironing board

iron

garbage can

dish soap

dishcloth

tablecloth

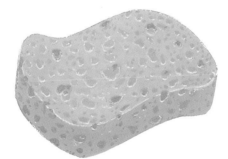

sponge

place mat

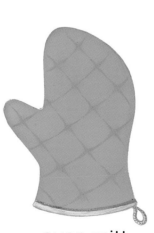

oven mitt

apron

IN THE BROOM CLOSET

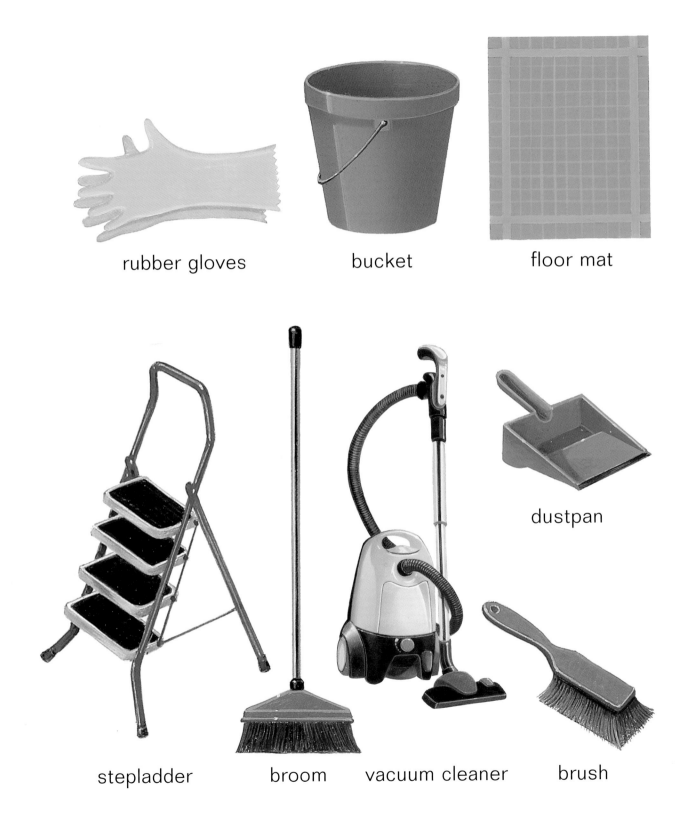

rubber gloves

bucket

floor mat

stepladder

broom

vacuum cleaner

dustpan

brush

sewing machine   thimble   spool of thread   needle

tray   lightbulb   battery   button

suitcase   travel bag   grocery cart

THE GARAGE

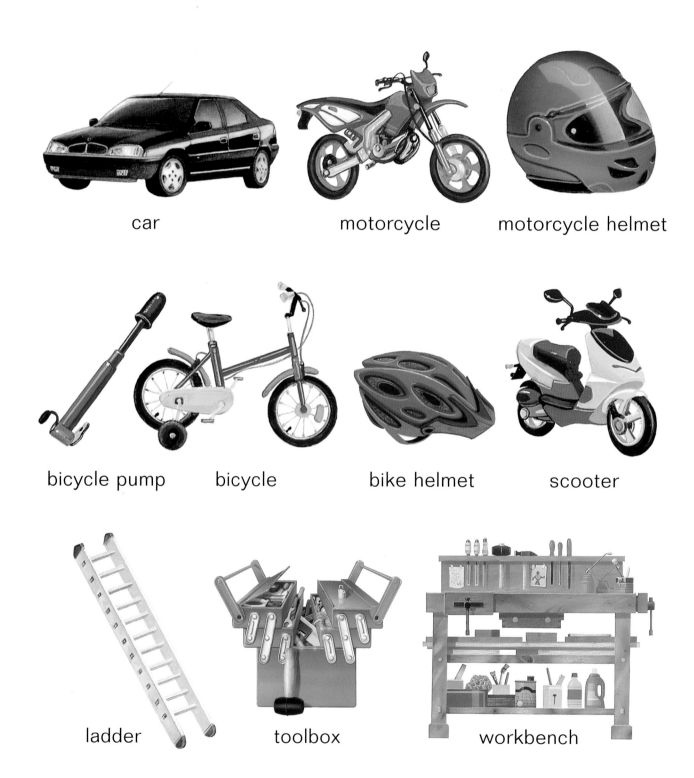

car

motorcycle

motorcycle helmet

bicycle pump

bicycle

bike helmet

scooter

ladder

toolbox

workbench

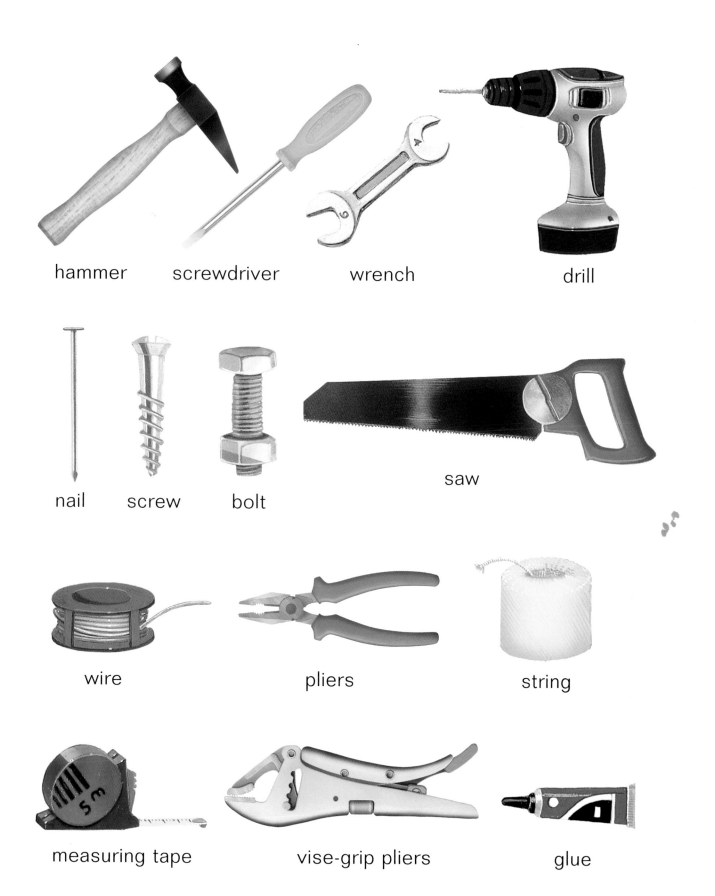

hammer   screwdriver   wrench   drill

nail   screw   bolt   saw

wire   pliers   string

measuring tape   vise-grip pliers   glue

IN THE GARDEN

dirt

grass

hedge

apple tree

cherry tree

orange tree

lime tree

tulip

rose

daisy

dahlia

peony

greenhouse

lawn mower

wheelbarrow

watering can

garden hose

clippers

iris

daffodil

flowerpot

shovel

pick

chalkboard

chalk

backpack

calendar

drawing

poster

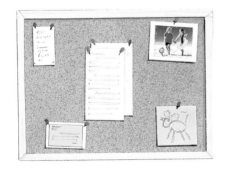

bulletin board

notebook

sheet of paper

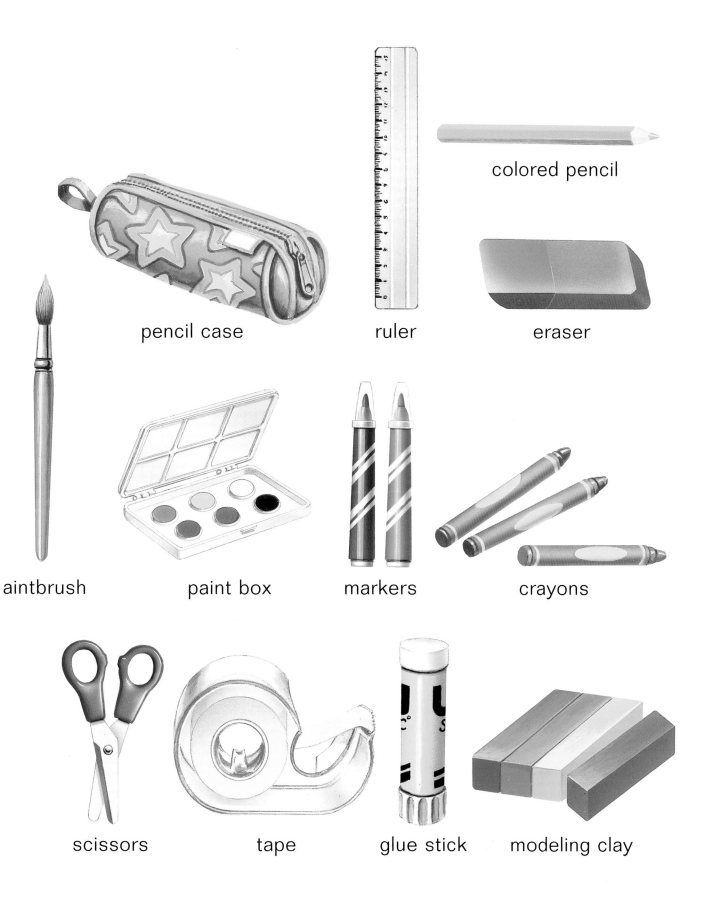

colored pencil

pencil case

ruler

eraser

aintbrush

paint box

markers

crayons

scissors

tape

glue stick

modeling clay

xylophone

harmonica

accordion

maracas

triangle

tambourine

castanets

cymbals

drum

drum set

guitar

violin

bow

cello

piano

sheet music

recorder

trumpet

saxophone

panpipes

trapeze   rings   stilts   rope

ball   baseball   bat   soccer ball

gym mat   basketball

ballet slippers

Question

What surface is good for doing somersaults?

Answer: a gym mat

tutu

sneakers

tracksuit

cleats

uniform shirt

uniform shorts

TRANSPORTATION

bus

subway car

car

school bus

truck

garbage truck

police car

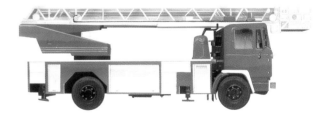

fire truck

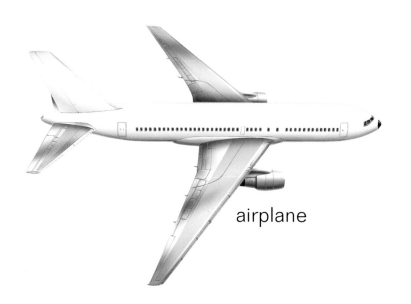

airplane

D i d   y o u   k n o w ?

Cement mixers have to keep turning so that the cement inside doesn't get too hard to pour out.

locomotive   train car

backhoe loader   bulldozer

ambulance   cement mixer

THE PARK

bench

paper boat

bucket

rake

shovel

pool

sandbox

sieve

mold

sand sculpture

marbles

40

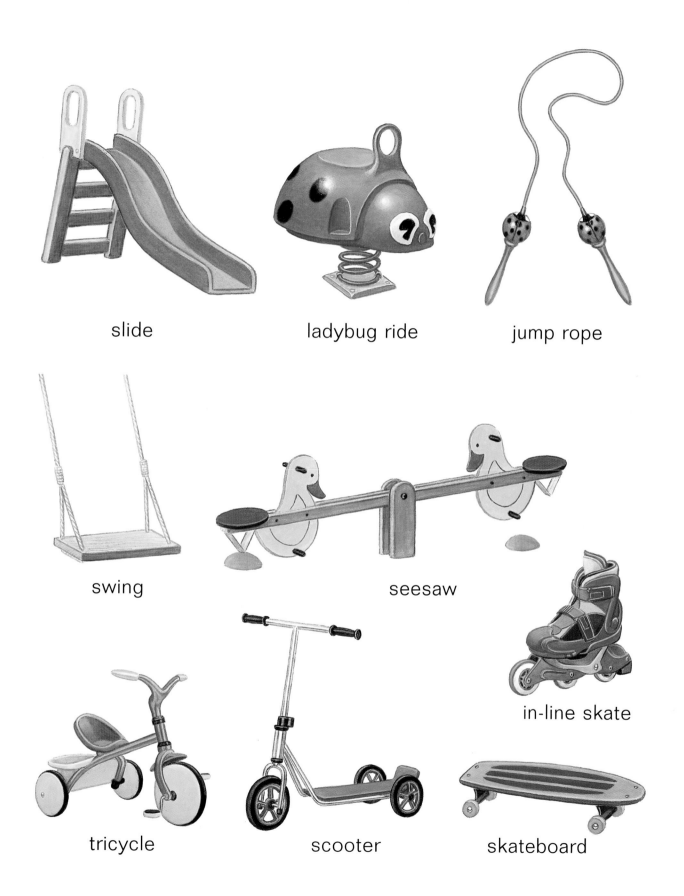

slide

ladybug ride

jump rope

swing

seesaw

in-line skate

tricycle

scooter

skateboard

THE ZOO

polar bear

panda

koala

fence

swamp

pond

birdhouse

zoo guard

monkey island

bear corner

lion cage

kangaroo and joey

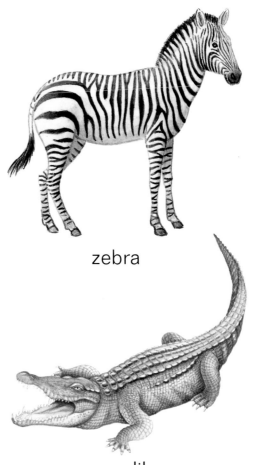

zebra

crocodile

THE ZOO

lion

tiger

jaguar

black panther

dromedary

camel

giraffe

ostrich

parrot

toucan

penguin
and chick

sea lion

seal

turtle

chimpanzee

monkey

gorilla

FOOD

salt

pepper

mustard

egg

meat

fish

hot dog

salami

ham

vinegar   oil   water

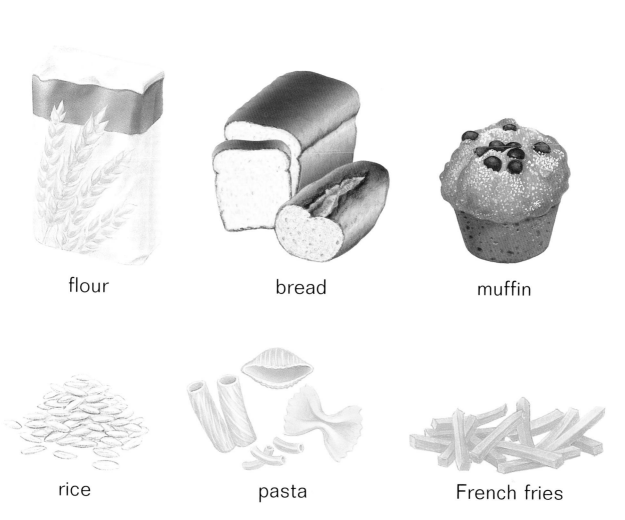

flour   bread   muffin

rice   pasta   French fries

FOOD

coffee beans

tea

orange juice

milk

cheese

yogurt

butter

pizza

sandwich

hamburger

peanut butter   sugar   honey   jelly

oatmeal   cookies

cereal

fruit pie   chocolate   chocolate cake

VEGETABLES

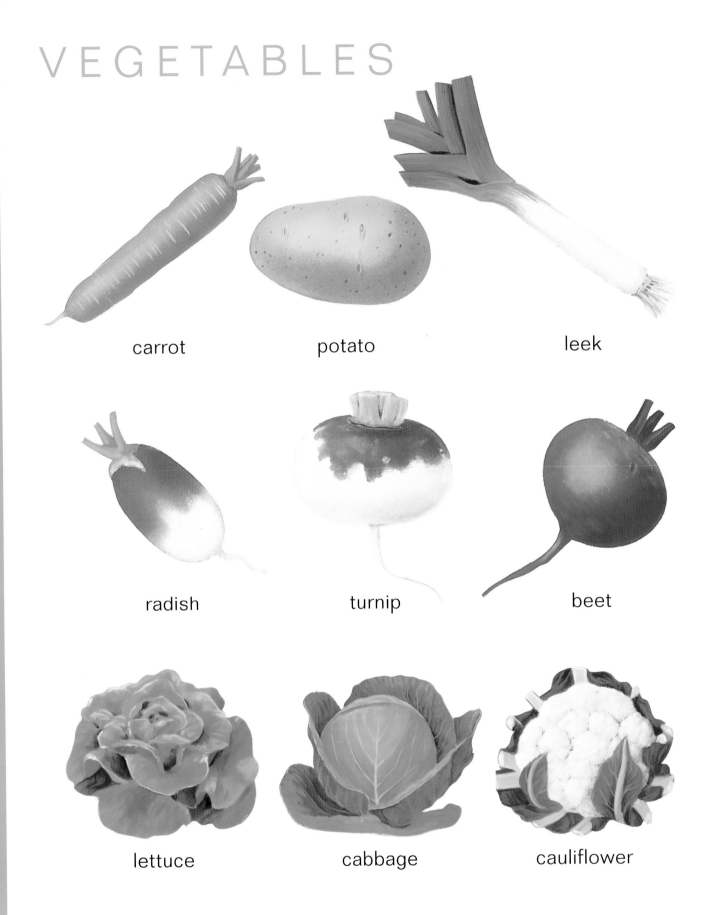

carrot

potato

leek

radish

turnip

beet

lettuce

cabbage

cauliflower

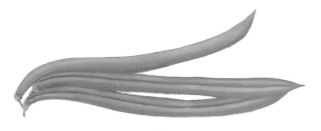

green beans

Did you know?

Peas come in a case called a pod. You don't eat the pod.

Taking the peas out of the pod is called "shelling peas."

peas

Brussels sprouts

spinach

broccoli

artichoke

endive

VEGETABLES

eggplant

bell pepper

chili pepper

zucchini

cucumber

sweet potato

onion

garlic

shallot

mushroom

pumpkin

Question

Which
vegetables
do you
like to eat?

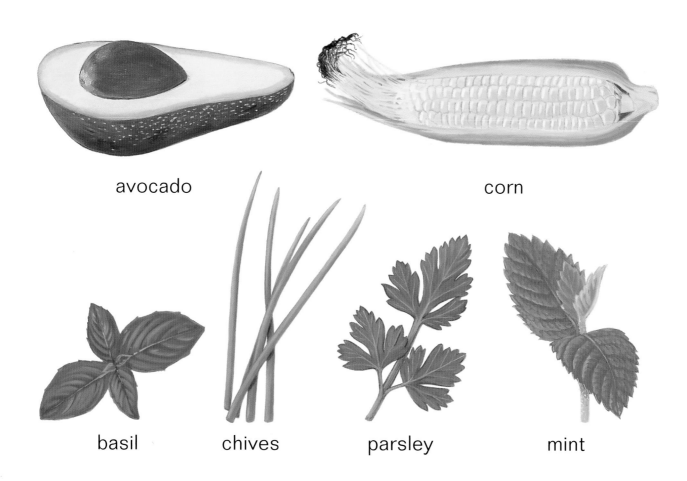

avocado

corn

basil

chives

parsley

mint

FRUITS

tomato

strawberry

cherry

raspberry

red currants

black currants

blueberries

blackberry

fig

D i d   y o u   k n o w ?

Even though many people think tomatoes are vegetables, they're actually fruits. Tomato sauce, salsa, and ketchup are all made with tomatoes.

apricot

peach

plum

lemon

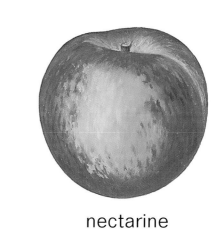

nectarine

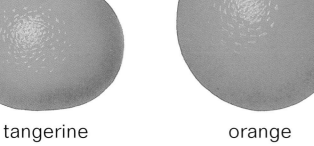

tangerine

orange

grapefruit

apple

pear

banana

grapes

kiwi

melon

hazelnut

walnut

chestnut

star fruit   papaya   mango   watermelon

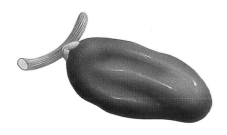

date

coconut

Did you know?

A chestnut has a prickly covering called a bur.

pineapple

IN THE FOREST

burrow

nest

pinecone

bud

leaf

acorn

bramble

fern

holly

oak

fir

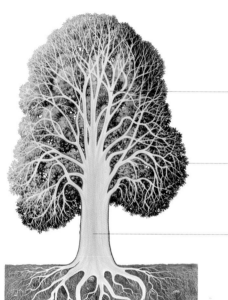

branch

leaves

trunk

root

birch

willow

chestnut

poplar

IN THE FOREST

Question

Which animal carries its house on its back?

Answer: the snail

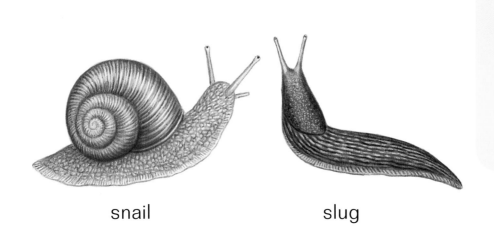

snail   slug

Did you know?

The owl stays awake all night and sleeps during the day.

hedgehog   lizard

owl   pheasant   woodpecker

squirrel

hare

badger

wolf

fox

wild boar

deer

stag

bat

stork

partridge

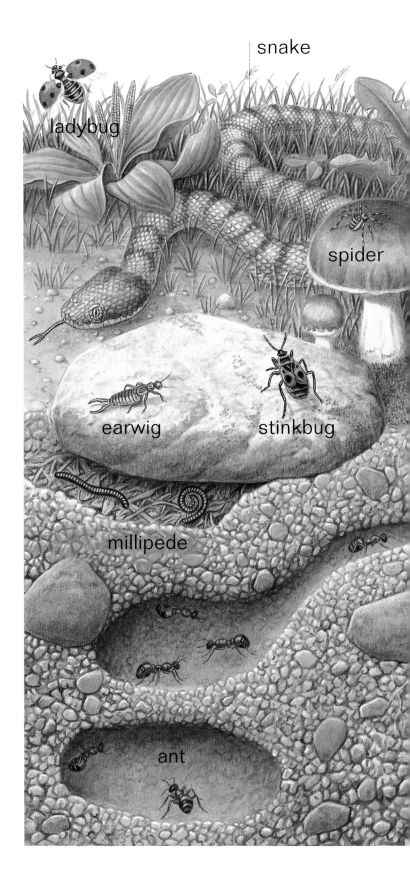

snake

ladybug

spider

earwig

stinkbug

millipede

ant

field mouse

stag beetle

earthworm

mole

swallow

magpie

sparrow

robin

jay

blackbird

blue tit

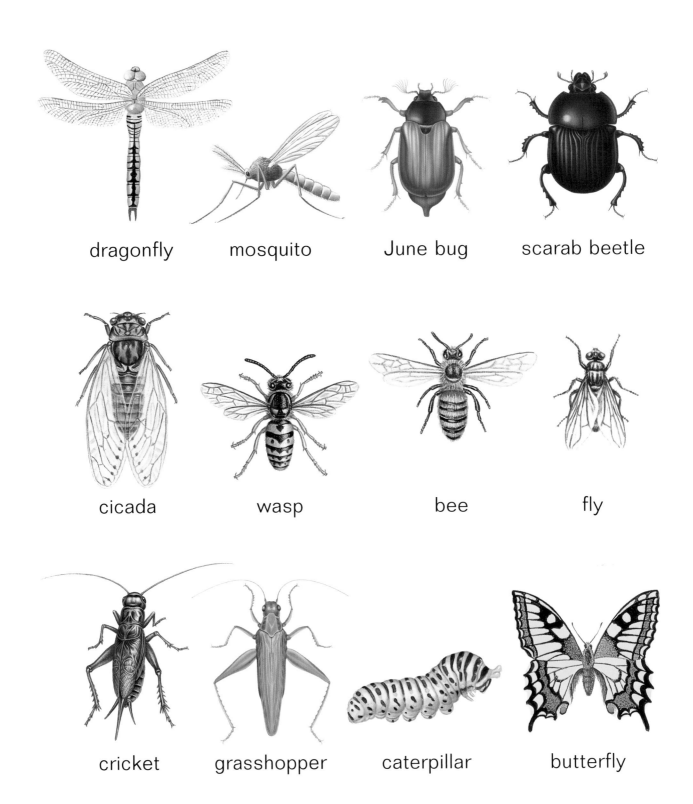

dragonfly   mosquito   June bug   scarab beetle

cicada   wasp   bee   fly

cricket   grasshopper   caterpillar   butterfly

mallard

duckling and duck

swan

kingfisher

moorhen

beaver

trout

frog

toad

CAMPING

tent

camper

trailer

hiking boots

binoculars

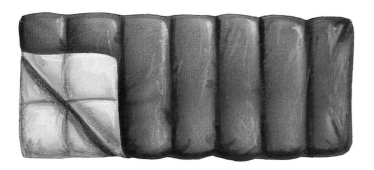

sleeping bag

Question

What should you do to stop a tent from blowing away in the wind?

Answer: Hammer tent stakes into the ground.

knapsack

compass

camera

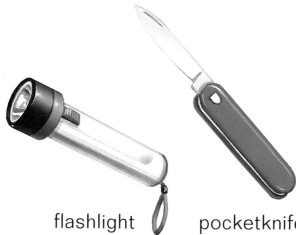

flashlight

pocketknife

camp stove

flask

pitchfork

bale of hay

rake

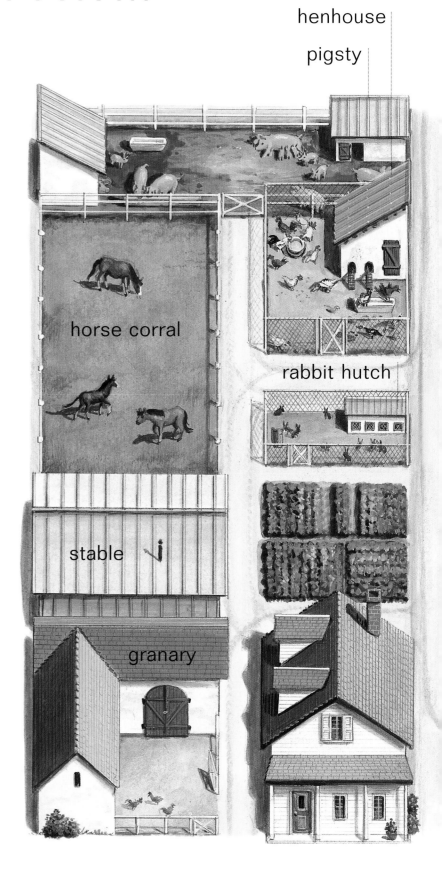

henhouse

pigsty

horse corral

rabbit hutch

stable

granary

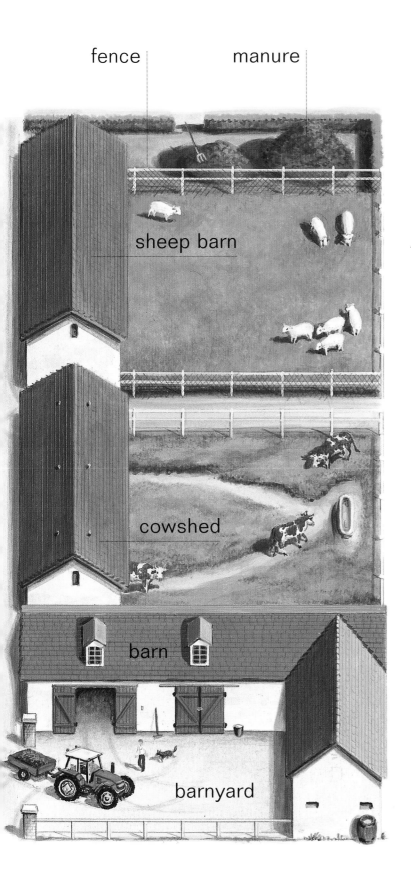

fence   manure

sheep barn

cowshed

barn

barnyard

tractor

combine harvester

plow

ON THE FARM

rooster, hen, and chick

duck

goose

turkeys

guinea fowl

cat and kitten

rabbit

70

horse and colt   donkey and foal

dog and puppy

cow and calf

pig and piglet

goat and kid

sheep and lamb

BY THE SEA

steamship

rock

pebble

seagull

island

sail

lighthouse

pier

harbor

cliff

beach

wave

jetty

mast

wharf

fishing boat

anchor

seaweed

BY THE SEA

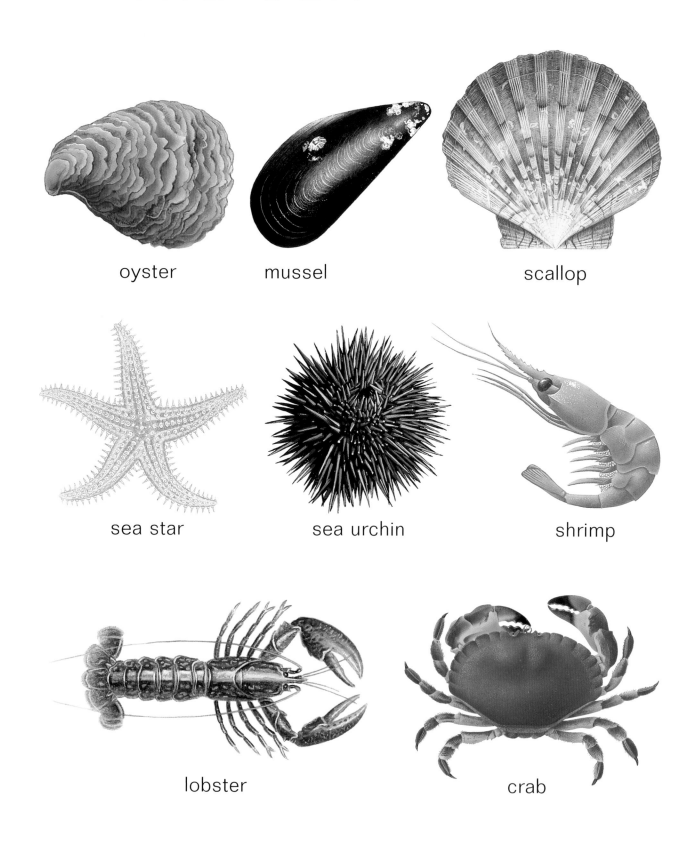

oyster

mussel

scallop

sea star

sea urchin

shrimp

lobster

crab

Did you know?

The blue whale is the biggest animal in the world.

It lives in the sea, but it's not a fish. It's a mammal like you!

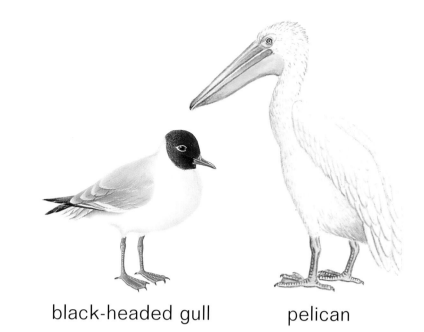

black-headed gull   pelican

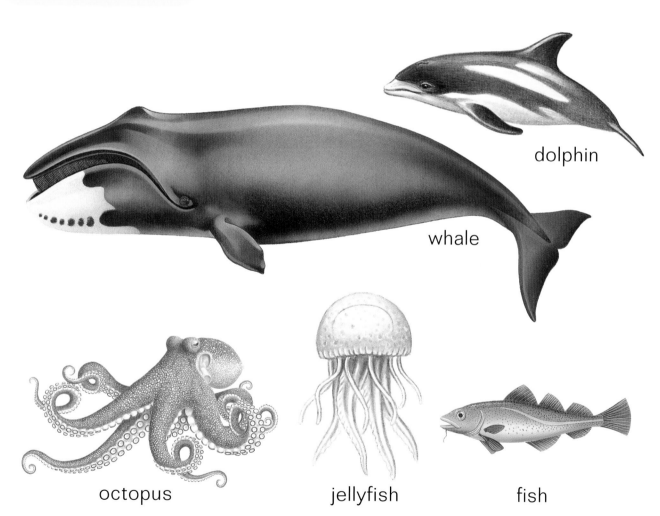

dolphin

whale

octopus   jellyfish   fish

BY THE SEA

beach towel

beach chair

umbrella

sunblock

swimsuits

sunglasses

sun hat

kite

Activity

Find all the objects that help protect you from the sun.

Answer: the sun hat, the sunglasses, the sunblock, and the umbrella

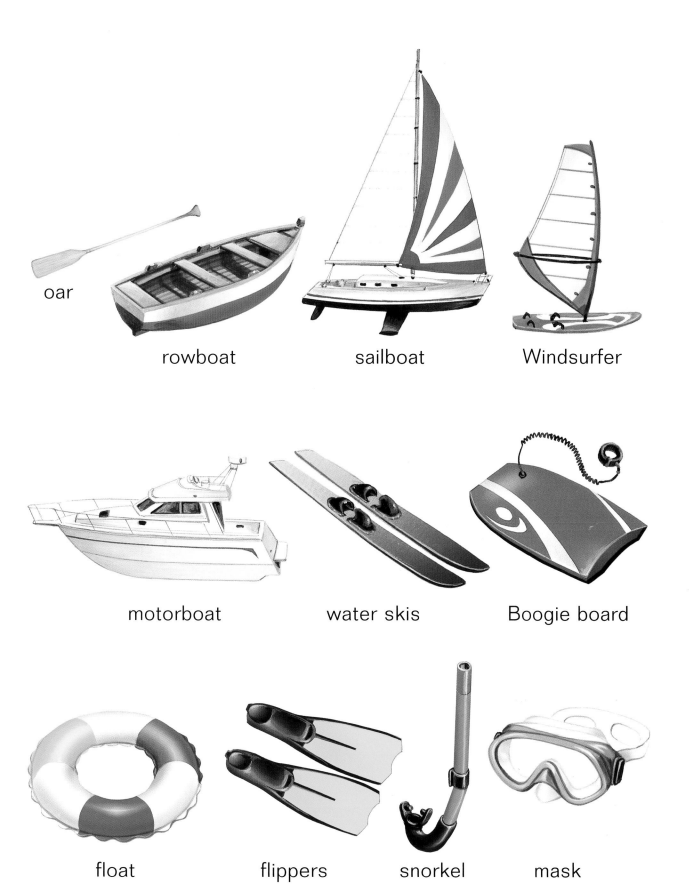

oar

rowboat

sailboat

Windsurfer

motorboat

water skis

Boogie board

float

flippers

snorkel

mask

IN THE MOUNTAINS

eagle

grackle

woodchuck

edelweiss

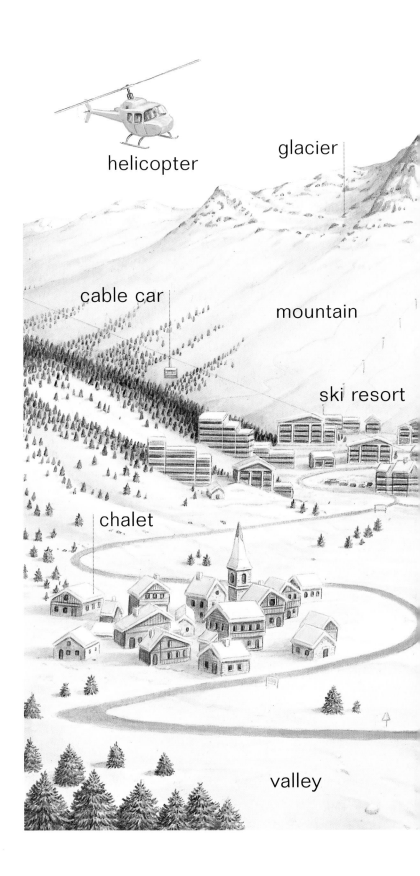

helicopter

glacier

cable car

mountain

ski resort

chalet

valley

summit

ski lift

tunnel

lake

dam

snow

snowplow

bridge

Saint Bernard

bear and bear cub

mountain goat

bighorn mountain
sheep

mittens

ski hat

face mask

ski mask

ski boots

ski suit

snowboard

snowshoes

skis

hang glider

parachute

hot-air balloon

ski poles

ice ax

climbing rope

carabiner

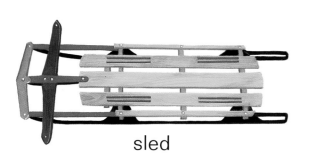

sled

Question

What lets you soar
through the sky like
a bird without
making any noise?

Answer: a hang glider

Index

a
b
c
d
e
f
g
h
i
j
k
l
m
n
o
p
q
r
s
t
u
v
w
x
y
z

a
b
c
d
e
f
g
h
i
j
k
l
m
n
o
p
q
r
s
t
u
v
w
x
y
z

a
b
c
d
e
f
g
h
i
j
k
l
m
n
o
p
q
r
s
t
u
v
w
x
y
z

a
b
c
d
e
f
g
h
i
j
k
l
m
n
o
p
q
r
s
t
u
v
w
x
y
z

a
b
c
d
e
f
g
h
i
j
k
l
m
n
o
p
q
r
s
t
u
v
w
x
y
z

a
b
c
d
e
f
g
h
i
j
k
l
m
n
o
p
q
r
s
t
u
v
w
x
y
z

a
b
c
d
e
f
g
h
i
j
k
l
m
n
o
p
q
r
s
t
u
v
w
x
y
z

a
b
c
d
e
f
g
h
i
j
k
l
m
n
o
p
q
r
s
t
u
v
w
x
y
z